THE GREAT South Yorkshire FLOODS

THE STORY IN PICTURES OF THE AREA'S BIGGEST CIVIL EMERGENCY IN OVER 50 YEARS

at heart  publications

Doncaster **Free Press**   **Times** South Yorkshire   **Guardian**

First published in 2007 by:
At Heart Ltd, 32 Stamford Street,
Altrincham, Cheshire, WA14 1EY

In conjunction with
The Doncaster Free Press
South Yorkshire Times
Workshop Guardian

Printed by Bell & Bain, Scotland.

ISBN: 978-1-84547-178-1

CONTENTS

INTRODUCTION

IT started out as yet another dark, rainy day in the washout of a summer 2007 but within hours it was clear that Monsoon Monday – as it became known – was the start of the biggest civil emergency in Doncaster since 1947.

Then, as now, it was the area's susceptibility to flooding that sparked alarm, as river levels rose and drains overflowed sending murky water rushing into hundreds of homes forcing families to flee.

Monday, June 25:

Chief Inspector Nick Whitehouse, the senior police officer in charge of the Doncaster district, surveyed the falling rain from his district headquarters in Scawsby.

As the morning progressed and the rain continued to fall, the first reports of localised flooding started to come in. Very quickly it became apparent that these were more than just isolated pockets of flooding. By 11am Chief Inspector Whitehouse took the decision to launch Silver Command, which brought together the borough's crisis management team.

There were real fears that the dam at Ulley Reservoir on the outskirts of Rotherham would burst sending a torrent of water all the way up the Don Valley to Doncaster and as far downstream as Stainforth. Police visited homes along the river from Mexborough to Stainforth warning residents of the potential danger.

With flood alerts already in place because of standing water from heavy rain earlier in the month, a further 80 millimetres of rain in one day meant the situation quickly deteriorated.

The A630 Doncaster to Rotherham road was closed, along with the A631 from Tickhill to Maltby. Rail and bus services were hit. By the end of the afternoon more than 20 schools had decided to close.

The first evacuations started with people moving out of their homes in Adwick, Bentley, Conisbrough and Mexborough.

Tuesday, June 26:

The horrific scale of the crisis became known. Families were roused from their beds to be evacuated as the flood waters rose to danger levels. Thousands of people from 60 streets across Auckley, Barnby Dun, Bentley, Conisbrough, Fishlake, Mexborough, Sprotbrough and Stainforth were taken to six council-run rest centres, others opted to move in with family or friends. Firefighters from across the country were drafted in to help fight the rising waters. Engineers and emergency workers were still at Ulley desperately working to save the dam.

Wednesday, June 27:

Twelve severe flood warnings were now in place around Doncaster, mainly for the River Don itself and the Ea Beck stream that runs through the villages to the north.

The army had been drafted in as rising waters threatened an electricity sub-station at Thorpe Marsh, near Barnby Dun, that supplies most of the power to Doncaster town centre. An RAF Chinook helicopter lifted tonnes of aggregate to shore up the Don's flood defences at Almholme Lane, Arksey.

Police divers were searching for a man reported to have fallen into a swollen dyke near Adwick-le-Street. The operation was called off hours later when it emerged that it had been a false alarm.

The evacuations gathered pace with more than 180 people rescued from Toll Bar. Other areas now affected included Thorpe in Balne, Sykehouse and Scawthorpe.

There were more road closures, including the A19, which was to remain closed for several weeks, parts of the A638 at Bawtry and the A630 at Balby. Rail services to Leeds were not operating. Thirty-four primary schools and four secondary schools were now closed

Thursday, June 28:

The first – and only – fatality related to the floods in the Doncaster area was reported. A 63-year-old man died when he fell into the Fossdyke

Canal at Torksey, near Gainsborough. The threat from Ulley dam has now abated. River levels were falling, but more rain was forecast.

Firefighters from across the country manning high-volume pumps worked round the clock to rid areas like Bentley High Street and Toll Bar of the standing water still evident on the streets.

Nine days after the rain fell, the Prince of Wales visited Toll Bar. The village was still under several feet of water and the Prince took to an inflatable boat to tour the area.

Almost 300 residents, mainly of Toll Bar, remained in council rest centres, with more staying with family or friends. By mid July a camp for people labelled "environmental refugees" had been set up in Toll Bar. The road to recovery had begun. But a return to normality was still a long way off with many families expecting to be living in mobile homes for 12 to 18 months.

And whether Toll Bar's ruined homes are to be rebuilt on the flood plain that has seen the area devastated twice in 50 years remains to be seen.

South Yorkshire Times

Thursday, June 21, 2007 — Serving the community since 1877 — www.southyorkshiretimes.co.uk — 32p

WIN £500 to spend on a new bathroom
At Bathstore Barnsley - see p15

WIN family day out at Legoland
Leisure competition - p11

Prom photo special inside
Northcliffe and Mexborough - p17

■ 36-PAGE PROPERTY GUIDE   ■ 24-PAGE MOTOR GUIDE   ■ TV PAGE 12   ■ SPORT STARTS PAGE 33

TAKE TO THE HILLS

Reader Louise Weigold sent in this photograph of Cliff Road, Darfield, showing how stranded residents resorted to unusual means to get around.

TODAY is traditionally the first day of summer - but torrential rainfall has brought about our area's worst floods in living memory.

Darfield was worst hit, with about 150 homes affected by flooding and some residents needing to be evacuated by boat in the early hours of Saturday.

One resident rescued from her bungalow by firefighters told the South Yorkshire Times: "It was like wild rapids."

Yesterday South Yorkshire's fire crews were at full stretch pumping water out of flooded properties in Wath, Swinton and Rawmarsh, and people whose homes were flooded at the weekend were returning to find out how many of their possessions had survived the deluge.

With more heavy rain predicted in the week to come, the Environment Agency still had flood watches in place for the River Dearne and the River Don as we went to press and the area was bracing itself for the possibility of more floods in the coming days.
SPECIAL REPORT: PAGES 3, 4 & 5

Inside this week:

Man rescued from chip pan fire
A MEXBOROUGH man had a lucky escape after an unattended chip pan sparked a blaze at his home. - p2

Wedding washout for unhappy couple
NEWLYWEDS Simon and Gillian Barnes couldn't have picked a worse day to get married, but put on a brave face after their wedding venue was flooded. - p3

Controversial TARA chair quits over 'bully' claim
COMMUNITY worker Sean Gibbons has resigned from his position after being accused of bullying by a local councillor. - p7

Wath's new swimming pool plans unveiled
AN artist's impression of a new leisure centre to be built in Wath has been revealed. - p7

Teacher on shortlist for national award
A PRIMARY school teacher will learn whether he has bagged the prestigious Teacher of the Year gong. - p9

▲
Cars struggle through water on Leger Way.

▶

The Fire Service conducted safety
checks at the *Doncaster Free Press*
offices on Sunny Bar after the heavy
rain caused leaks to the listed building.

▲

Cars struggle to get through the floods on Doncaster Road, Kirk Sandall.

◄

Many streets in Scawthorpe suffered due to the heavy rain. Cars were brought to a standstill here on Petersgate.

▲
Many drivers
struggled across
Doncaster to get
through the flooded
roads.

►

York Road, at the
junction with Barnsley
Road, was closed after
heavy rain caused
chaos in and around
Doncaster.

◀ Barnsley Road was closed.

▼

Residents of Mayfield Avenue, Stainforth, found their houses flooded. Ian Thompson, and John Bower and his wife Denise are pictured almost knee-deep in water.

Stainforth resident Keith Manning pictured outside his house on Mayfield Avenue.

Friends Jessica Duckitt and Leanne Bower take time out for a bit of fun.

▲
Walkers Garden
Centre, Auckley,
flooded during
the downpour.

▶
Home owners on
Maple Drive,
Auckley, had to
barricade their
houses with
sandbags.

Fighting the floods: resident Dave Weston and his friend Mick Lee barricade their house in Auckley.

▲
Neighbours Pete Neale (left)
and Mick Gatt work together
to bail out water from their
homes on Maple Drive,
Auckley.

▶

Jean and Brian Townend, of
Maple Drive, Auckley, were
stranded in their own home
after the storms on Monday
June 25.

▲
High water on
Swinton Road
between
Mexborough and
Swinton.

◄
A woman calls for
help from her car
after it cut out in
flood water on
Sheffield Road,
Conisbrough.

▲ Children watch as cars struggle through flood water on Sheffield Road, Conisbrough.

▶ Passers-by push a stranded car out of flood water on Sheffield Road, Conisbrough.

▲
A car struggles through flood water on Pastures Road, Mexborough.

◄

A family of seven from Clevedon Crescent, Scawthorpe, was evacuated to the Regent Hotel for a week. Left to right are Daniel Strutt, nine, dad Adam, Kyle, three, Lily-Mai, nine-months, Jack, seven, Luke, five, mum Debbie, and Gary Job, of the Association of Insurance Building Contractors which helped them to move.

▲

Farmer David Chappell had to resort to alternative means of transportation to feed some of his livestock after they got stranded when floods engulfed his land. Cows and sheep were cut off after the River Torne near Boston Park Farm in Hatfield Woodhouse burst its banks.

Mr Chappell, who has farmed the land for 32 years, made twice daily visits by dinghy to ensure the animals were fed and watered until the levels subsided. The family lost an estimated £60,000 worth of crops after farmland the size of 40 football pitches was submerged.

Mr Chappell is pictured with Scunthorpe United player and friend Andrew Butler.

◄

A brave Scawthorpe family rescued people from their flooded homes on Petersgate, in their grandad's boat, after the torrential rain. Left to right are Ray Bucknell, 51, Daniel Baxter, 14, Ben Myatt, 26, brother Richard, 33, and niece Martine Hellewell, 15.

The River Don burst its banks after severe rain, flooding parts of Marshgate and Bentley.

▲ The aftermath of the River Don bursting its banks.

▲ Caravans next to St George's Bridge were evacuated during the flood.

◄

People wade through knee-deep water with bin bags full of essentials, as they leave their mobile homes.

▲

Residents on Hunt
Lane, Bentley, wade
through the water
with supplies after
their street flooded
badly when the
River Don burst its
banks during the
severe rain.

▶

Torrents of water
stream down
Marshgate.

Under water: the area between Yarborough Terrace and Marshgate.

▲
Yarborough Terrace,
Bentley.

▶

Cars are stranded at the
site.

▲
This familiar terrace in Bentley is almost unrecognisable.

◄

Police and the Fire Service were on hand on Tuesday June 26 after the old North Bridge flooded.

▲
Council workers
load up sandbags
ready for
despatch.

▶

Emergency
services pictured
on standby as
the River Don
overflows at
Marshgate.

▲

Sprotbrough Road, at the Junction with York Road is closed after heavy rain caused it to flood.

◄

Water from the River Don sweeps through houses and businesses at North Bridge, Doncaster.

Castle Hills Primary School was flooded after the heavy rain.

Pupils had to stay at home after water engulfed their school.

▲

Danesway, Scawthorpe, shown here and opposite, flooded after heavy rain.

▶

Mandy Lumsden and her six children had to be evacuated to Don Valley High School after their street Danesway, in Scawthorpe flooded. Mandy is pictured here with three of her children. Left to right are Gabrielle, 13, Courtney, ten and Charlie, two.

Kim Evison, 43, of Danesway, Scawthorpe, surveys the damage to her home.

▲
Sprotbrough Road,
at the junction
with York Road.

◄
Bentley resident,
Glen Robinson, 28,
tries to make his
way to dry land.

Kirk Sandall railway station. These three pictures are taken looking towards Stainforth, two from the platform and next page, from the bridge.

◄

Council staff
rescuing people
from their homes
in Home
Meadows, Tickhill.

▲

Cars forge
through the
waters on Leger
Way.

▶

Water levels
continued to rise
in Tickhill.

Worksop Road,
Tickhill.

Locals don't let the flood waters stop them from taking a walk in Tickhill.

Tickhill floods.

▲
Tickhill streets
running with
water.

▶
Water Lane,
Tickhill.

◄

Tickhill floods.

▼

Great North Road,
Scawthorpe,
Doncaster.

▲

Asken Road,
Bentley,
Doncaster.

▶

Watch House
Lane, Bentley,
Doncaster.

▲

Pipering Lane –
middle part,
Scawthorpe,
Doncaster.

◄

Amersall Road,
Scawthorpe,
Doncaster.

▲   A630 Conisbrough.

◄

Low Road in Conisbrough.

▲ Flood water around Dearne Valley Leisure Centre.

◀

Tickhill floods.

Flooded railway tracks leading into Mexborough. Picture taken from the bridge between Mexborough and Denaby Main.

◀

Martine Hellewell, 15, helps rescue a dog from the floods on Petersgate, Scawthorpe.

▼

Hexthorpe Park. The river flooded up past the rowing club.

Thorpe Marsh Power Station is the scene of a major clear up after emergency services work against the clock to stop water from getting into the mains.

Toll Bar.

▲
Wheatley Hall
Road on right.

◄
River Don with the
A1 in the
foreground.

▲
Scawthorpe –
Castle Hills
School.

Above
Hexthorpe.

South Yorkshire Times

Thursday, June 28, 2007 — Serving the community since 1877 — www.southyorkshiretimes.co.uk — 32p

Flood stories and photographs
See pages 2, 4 and 5

Vandals target castle again
Misery at tea rooms- p7

Meet Dearne's Billy Elliot!
Dancing king - p3

■ 40-PAGE PROPERTY GUIDE ■ 28-PAGE MOTOR GUIDE ■ TV PAGE 12 ■ SPORT STARTS PAGE 33

COME HELL AND HIGH WATER

County in crisis after a second week of floods

SOUTH Yorkshire is today beginning its long journey back to normality after the worst floods in living memory.

While Sheffield, which has seen the worst of the bad weather, remains in crisis, the situation elsewhere in the county is beginning to ease.

Many of the major roads which were closed due to the flooding, including Low Road in Conisbrough and Doncaster Road in Denaby Main, have now re-opened.

And residents of Conisbrough and Mexborough who were evacuated from their homes have been allowed back.

But there still remains the risk that the Ulley reservoir near Rotherham could burst, which would have devastating knock-on effects for towns and villages along the River Don.

● For more on the flooding, see pages 2, 4 and 5.

YOUR LOCAL MOBILITY DEALER
NEVER BEATEN ON PRICE OR SERVICE Local friendly staff serving local people in and about the community THOUSANDS OF EVERYDAY PRODUCTS

RISER CHAIRS   STAIR LIFTS   SCOOTERS   BATH LIFTS   WIDE FITTING SHOES & SLIPPERS

Your local Branch
PARKGATE MOBILITY
Effingham Street, Rotherham
01709 378909
DONCASTER MOBILITY
High Street, Bentley
01302 822099
BARNSLEY MOBILITY
Doncaster Road, Barnsley
01226 281111

---

www.doncasterfreepress.co.uk

...ress

55p

Race for life P34

...ge ...quits
...visit - P8

■ JOBS START PAGE 56 ■ WEEKEND TV - PAGE 42

...exthorpe, looking towards Doncaster town centre, taken by Andy Young

Another weather warning as town tries to cope with worst flood in decades

IT'S NOT OVER YET

Turn to page 2

Glycolic Skin Peels
Colonic Hydrotherapy
Restylane Dermal Fillers
C.A.C.E Non Surgical Facelift
Wrinkle Reduction Treatment
Elemis Face & Body Treatments
Spa Find Face & Body Treatments
Jan Marini Skin Care Management
Microdermabrasion & Glycolic Facials
Hair Reduction & Skin Rejuvenation
Endermologie (Cellulite Reduction)
Manicures & Pedicures
Spa Day Packages
Holistic Therapies

We are proud to introduce 'VISIA™ Complexion Analysis System'

It is now possible to record surface and subsurface skin conditions: wrinkles, spots, pores, evenness, sun damage. So we are able to offer 'YOU' the best possible advice & treatments tailor made to suit your skin.

The first 20 clients presenting this advert will receive FREE analysis and advice.

Elemis fIND

'Have 2 Bars' Offers
(valid until the end of Sept 07)
Buy...Luxury Pedicure
Get...Manicure Free
Buy...Luxury Pedicure
Get...Manicure Free
Buy...Semi Permanent
Eye Lash Tint
Get...Semi Permanent Eye
Brow Tint or Shape
Spray Tans Only £10 every
Thursday & Friday

The Fountain
AT BARRINGTON HOUSE

Telephone
(01302) 370 270

10 Bawtry Road
Bessacarr, Doncaster

▲
Bentley High
Street was hit by
flood waters.

▶
Bentley residents
were evacuated
as flood waters
continued to
rise.

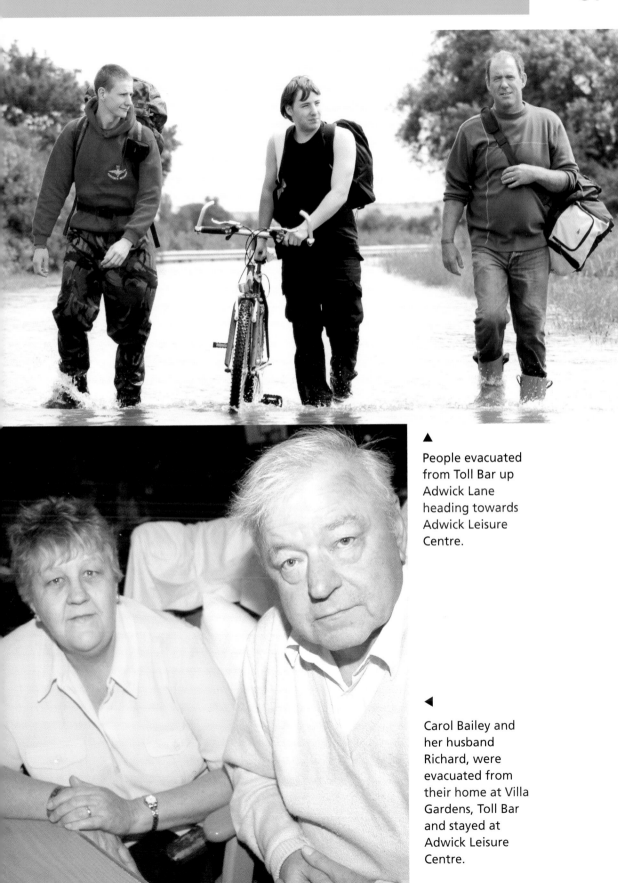

▲

People evacuated
from Toll Bar up
Adwick Lane
heading towards
Adwick Leisure
Centre.

◄

Carol Bailey and
her husband
Richard, were
evacuated from
their home at Villa
Gardens, Toll Bar
and stayed at
Adwick Leisure
Centre.

▲

Red Cross volunteers helped out at Adwick Leisure Centre. Pictured are (left to right) volunteer, Stephanie Grant, Ben Ellison, of Toll Bar, volunteers Lynn Stow, Chris Green, Sandra Vaughan and Dorothy Ellison, of Toll Bar.

▶

Doncaster Free Press reporter Chris Walker pictured surveying the damage at Bentley.

Cooke Street, Bentley, was badly affected by the floods.

▲

Flood water is
pumped off
Bentley High
Street.

▶

South Yorkshire
Police Tactical
Support Group get
kitted out to help
drain flood water
from Bentley High
Street.

▲
Lancashire Fire
Service Swift
Water Rescue
Team travelled to
Bentley to help
residents trapped
in their homes.
Left to right are
firefighters Martin
Rose, Alistair
Cudworth,
Anthony Palmer,
and Chris Wales.

◄
Finkle Street,
Bentley, amidst the
flood.

▲

Firefighters from all over the country helped to pump water from
Bentley. Left to right are Jim McNulty, Jim Picton and FC Squires.

◄

Bentley Library amidst the flood.

▲

Keith Wesley, 67,
was devastated
when his boat,
Merlin, was
submerged after a
torrent of water hit
Eastwood Lock,
Parkgate.

▶

Doncaster Town 'B'
Captain Mark
Dickinson pictured
shortly before his
team's game with
Wickersley was
called off.

▲
Jubilee Bridge, at Thorne, was heavily guarded with sandbags after reaching its highest ever point.

◄
Chris Hancock alongside his submerged narrow boat, *Dovetail* at Eastwood Lock, Parkgate.

CLEARING UP

It was only when the waters had finally gone, almost two weeks after the heavens had opened, that the massive clean-up operation could start.

For the first time, residents and the authorities surveyed the true cost of the devastation and the prospects did not provide much cheer. Over 30,000 homes and 7,000 businesses were thought to have been affected across South Yorkshire and insurance companies estimated the total cost of the region's damage to be close to £1 billion.

Nonetheless, with so much to do, the race to re-build homes, businesses and lives needed to begin straight away.

An emergency relief donation fund was quickly established by residents moved by the plight of their neighbours. Donations to the South Yorkshire Flood Relief Fund began pouring in to help the region's victims with their basic needs. After just two weeks, generous well-wishers had emptied their pockets to the tune of over £200,000, with donations still coming in.

For many residents however, before they could clear-up, they needed somewhere to stay.

The borough's emergency refuge centres at leisure and community centres which had housed over 350 people, were closing as normal life began to resume for those not affected. The remaining evacuees were directed to the disused £38 million Earth Centre in Conisbrough, but all who were sheltering said they simply wanted to return to their old lives and begin to re-build.

Father-of-three Pete Hobson took refuge there with his wife and young children. He said: "We walked into Adwick Leisure Centre with nothing but what we had on our backs. I appreciate what they're doing for us but it isn't quite a home. I don't want to be here for 12 months. It's going to be a big job when we do move back home but we'll get there. We'll get through it."

Meanwhile, as plans for the 'environmental refugee' camp began in earnest on the Manor Estate in Toll Bar, Mayor Martin Winter warned families not to under-estimate how long it would take to recover from the floods. Residents of the worst-hit homes were told by the mayor it might be up to 18 months before they could move back into their homes, if at all.

For other residents in the borough, life had slowly started to return to normal. The roads which had been impassable including North Bridge, York Road, Balby Road and routes around Bawtry, began to re-open one by one. Only the A19 at Toll Bar remained closed as August approached.

The dozens of schools which had shut after the downpour re-opened leaving just a handful still mopping-up as the summer holidays drew near.

For the flooded homeless, the first of many council-funded static caravans were delivered around the borough. Residents queued-up to be the first to return to live within their cherished communities.

Residents and volunteers started the arduous task of stripping houses of ruined furniture and carpets to allow the foundations and walls to dry out before repair work could begin.

Following Prince Charles' morale-boosting lead, the new Prime Minister Gordon

Brown arrived in Toll Bar on one of his first official visits in his new role. However, despite promising a £14 million rescue package for rebuilding and repairs, residents blasted the PM for not helping sooner.

Angry father-of-two David Howard was restrained by bodyguards from reaching Mr Brown. Shouting through the village hall windows, he said: "What has he come for? What are we actually getting? I'm a working man. I want help."

He added: "People on benefits are getting new houses and furniture but where's the help for honest hard-working tax payers?"

Other ministerial visits to the borough shortly followed. Ed Balls, the schools minister was given a guided tour of flood-hit Rosedale Primary in Scawsby and Castle Hills Primary in Scawthorpe. He promised to help the schools in their bid to re-open as normal in September. "Teachers, parents and children deserve no less", he said.

Environment Secretary Hilary Benn surveyed the damage to the north of the borough, accompanied by Doncaster North MP and cabinet office minister Ed Miliband. Mr Miliband vowed to support his constituents in the aftermath of the disaster, paying tribute to their "resilience and spirit."

Housing Minister Yvette Cooper also visited the Manor Estate in Toll Bar to see the full impact of the filthy water on the estate's homes. Taking a guided tour of Sharon Sanderson's rotting home where mould was quickly growing up the walls, she too pledged her support for residents.

As the weeks pass, the clean-up continues at a pace. Those affected are desperate to make progress before the autumn and the threat of more rain. Doncaster's residents know it will be a slow process, but together, with some of their famous unbreakable spirit, they are determined to return to their homes and the communities where they belong.

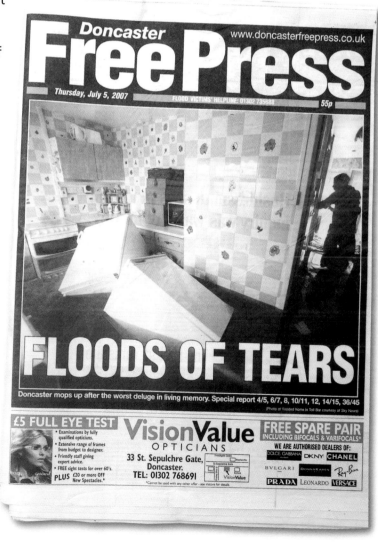

▲
Darius and Natasha Cooper in
their kitchen on Danesway,
Scawthorpe.

▶

Darius and Natasha Cooper look
out through a rain splashed
window at home in Scawthorpe.
Their house on Danesway was
badly hit by the recent floods.

Rob O'Brien from Campsall Working Men's Club delivering aid for flood victims to Adwick Leisure Centre.

▲

The Prince of Wales meets firefighters on his visit to the flooded streets of Toll Bar.

▶

The Prince of Wales boards a dinghy to tour the village.

▲
The Prince chats to emergency service workers.

◄
Toll Bar's sub-postmaster John Jackson accompanies the Prince during his visit.

▲
Toll Bar Primary School pupils in their underwater playground. Left to right are 11-year-olds Jessica Job, Nathan Didcott and Kieran Rodwell, who were back at their flooded school to be filmed by a BBC Newsround crew. Jessica said: "I'm upset about the school being closed. We'll be going to high school in September anyway but I'm sad that the school has been flooded."

▶
David Burnham, from West Midland's Fire Service takes a drinks break at Toll Bar. He said about the fire crew's work: "Progress is being made. We'll still be here for a while... the rugby pitch is still under water. We were the first crew to deploy the high volume pumping unit. The South Yorkshire Fire Brigade have been really looking after us with excellent hospitality."

▲
Local fitness instructor Julia Marshall, in her flood damaged property on Askern Road, Toll Bar. She said: "I'm staying with my parents now and my property is insured. I'm disappointed but I will return."

◄

View from the south end of Askern Road, Toll Bar.

▲
Andy Wilson, 20, outside his flooded home on Askern Road, Toll Bar. He said of the inside of his house: "It's all a mess. There's sludge everywhere and snails and worms in the house. The sofa's mouldy and it stinks. We're insured though."

►

Staff from D.M.B.C.'s community first team clear out flood damaged furniture and carpets from homes in Toll Bar.

◀

Rovers player Bruce Dyer signs an autograph for Iona Turner, 11, of Toll Bar, as the team visits flood victims staying at Adwick Leisure Centre.

▼

Rovers players take their prized Johnstone's Paint Trophy to show flood victims staying at Adwick Leisure Centre. Left to right are Adam Bacon, nine, of Toll Bar, Paul Heffernan, Lewis Guy, Jessica Job, 11, of Toll Bar, James Coppinger and James Job, seven, of Toll Bar.

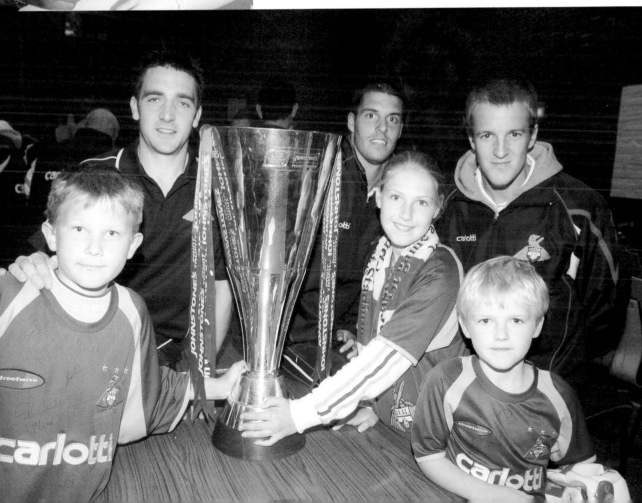

▶

Adam Bacon, nine, of Toll Bar, shares sweets with Rovers player Paul Green as the team visits flood victims staying at Adwick Leisure Centre.

▼

Mayor Martin Winter and Paul Hart, council manager, outline plans for dealing with the flood emergency plan in Doncaster during a press conference at the Council House.

▲
Fire Crews from across the country, who helped with the pumping operation gathered their equipment together at the Keepmoat Stadium ready to return home.

◄

Frank Parker and his son Graham Parker pictured outside their business, in Toll Bar.

▲
Linda Slack, manager of Mark Jarvis
bookmakers, in Bentley, pictured outside
the premises which have since re-opened.

▶
Toll Bar residents, Stuart and Michelle
Slack's house has been devastated by
the floods.

Many businesses suffered in the flooding at Bentley.

▲

The Salvation Army are handing out warm drinks and snacks to the residents and workers of Toll Bar.

▶

Manor Estate and Askern Road, Toll Bar, where residents are re-building their lives after their houses were wrecked by the floods.

▲
Heather Tomas, of
Manor Estate, Toll
Bar, starts to clean
up her home.

◄
Shocked residents
seek much-needed
advice.

▲

Jim Tyrer, of Bentley Top Club, has estimated it will take four to six months until the club can be re-opened after flood damage.

▶

The extent of the damage becomes clear in Bentley Top Club.

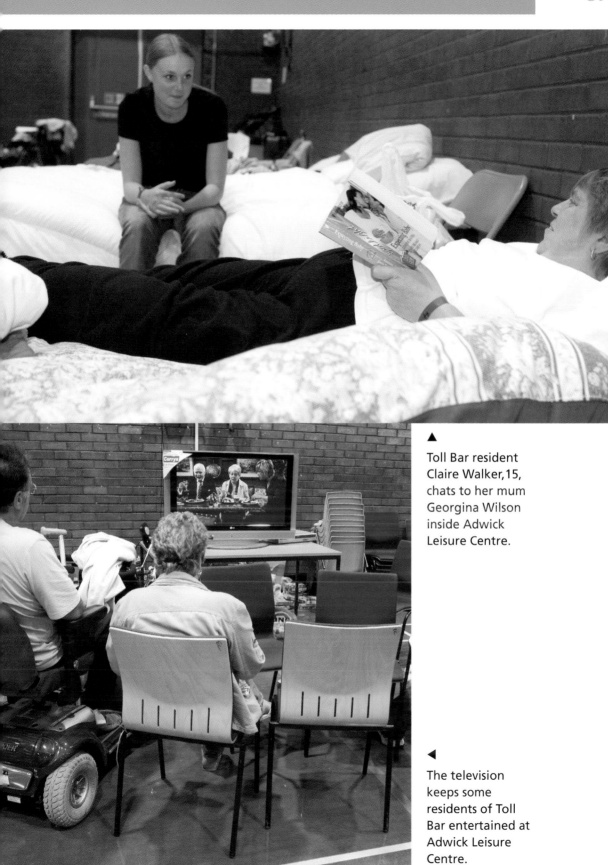

▲
Toll Bar resident Claire Walker,15, chats to her mum Georgina Wilson inside Adwick Leisure Centre.

◄
The television keeps some residents of Toll Bar entertained at Adwick Leisure Centre.

The main hall at Adwick Leisure Centre.

Doncaster Free Press

www.doncasterfreepress.co.uk

Thursday, July 12, 2007 | **INSIDE:** Pet Idol 2007 – your chance to vote *starts P41* | 55p

THE SLOW ROAD TO RECOVERY

The clean-up begins

- **Talks on refugee camp**
- **Pumping out finishes**
- **Insurance worries**
- **PM confronted on visit**

See pages 4, 5, 6, 7, 10, 11, 20, 21

Susan Bouse and daughter Julia Morris start cleaning up in Toll Bar.
(Picture: Liz Robinson D1383LR)

Ed Balls, MP and Secretary of State for Children, Schools and Families, visited Castle Hills Primary School, Scawthorpe, to see how the school coped during the flooding. He is pictured here talking to pupil Danny Hendry, six.

▲

Ed Balls is pictured here with (left to right) Ed Miliband, MP and Cabinet member, Martin Winter, Mayor of Doncaster and pupils Charlie Waugh, five and Joe Rose, six.

◄

The Styling Lounge, on Furlong Road, Bolton-upon-Dearne, held a coffee morning in aid of the South Yorkshire flood victims. Pictured back, from left are stylist Laura Buxton, Pamela Cartwright, of Furlong Road, and stylist Nikki Shaw. In front from left, are Laura Bedford, of Perfect 10, owner Lynne Wilkinson and Maggie Farr, of Furlong Road.

▲

Royal & SunAlliance Advice
Centre, Toll Bar.

▶

The Young family at home in
Adwick-Le Street. Their flood-hit
property was burgled twice.
Simon is pictured with one-year-
old Caitlyn and his wife Cheryl
holds two-week-old Charlie.

▲

Flood victims Linda and Ian Clark, of Askern Road, Toll Bar, have been put up in The Holiday Inn, Warmsworth, by their insurance company.

◄

Little baby Owen was born during the floods and is now safe at home in Bentley with mum Hayley Hensby, 18, and dad Chris Howard, 34.

▲

It's still raining: Flood victims on Northfield Road, Sprotbrough, have a street party to cheer themselves up, despite having to live in caravans. Left to right are Pauline Dunnill, of Sprotbrough Road, Georgina Hickman, Gail Cutts, Janet Wakefield, and husband Roy, and Rachel Mazey, all of Northfield Road.

▶

Lisa and Patrick Slack and their son Jack, pictured outside the caravan they were allocated as temporary accommodation while their house is repaired.

▲

People on the Manor Estate in Toll Bar have been allocated caravans to live in while their houses are renovated.

◄

Work gets under way to create a caravan park at the back of the Manor Estate, Toll Bar.

Doncaster Free Press

www.doncasterfreepress.co.uk

Thursday, July 26, 2007

55p

Town centre road race results

More than 400 competed in the annual challenge – Sport special Pages 74/75

More assaults on wardens

Traffic wardens and school workers bear the brunt of council staff violence – P7

At the centre of the storm

The team effort that saved lives in town's flood emergency – P36-45

■ 184 PAGES THIS WEEK   ■ JOBS START PAGE 58   ■ 20 PAGE MOTOR GUIDE   ■ 84 PAGES OF PROPERTY   ■ WEEKEND TV - PAGE 44

FEARS OVER GREEN WHEELIE WASTE

ONE third of Doncaster households are not using their green bins regularly - even at what should be the busiest time of the year, the Free Press has learned.

And council chiefs have admitted that the waste people are putting into their green bins is not fit to be used for compost, prompting fears that some could go to landfill. Garden waste and card that householders believe is being recycled is, in fact, being used for cleaning up derelict sites and as farm compost.

Concerned councillors are demanding more information on what is happening to the contents of the green bins now collected fortnightly across Doncaster.

Full Story - Page 11

Now things van only get better!

HOME FROM HOME: Lisa, Patrick Slack and their son Jack, outside their caravan while their house in Toll Bar is restored. The family are among scores of flood victims who have moved to a temporary caravan park - Special flood reports Pages 2/3, 4/5, 15, 36

Picture: MARIE CALEY D8256MC

INSIDE

More Asda jobs
THREE hundred people are already working at Asda's new national depot which opened this week, and 300 more are in the pipeline .
■ Page 12

Our Pet Idol champ
WHO'S a pretty boy then? Meet the winner of our popular Pet Idol competition.
■ Page 8

Sex pest jailed
A SEX beast who preyed on a vulnerable young man has been caged by a judge who warned that he was a danger to the public.
■ Page 22

Outcry over cuts
THERE was outrage as council finance bosses proposed shaving £1m from the borough's roads budget to help combat Doncaster's growing cash crisis.
■ Page 20

Brave cops honoured
A PAIR of brave police officers who arrested a machete-wielding sex offender after a car chase through Doncaster villages have been commended for their actions.
■ Page 12

SPORT

Fitness check
O'DRISCOLL to check on O'Connor's longer-term fitness after the right back had his first pre-season outing last night.
■ Back Page

Flood victim Marc Barkby, of Askern Road, Toll Bar, helps friend Ray Surgey deliver donated furniture to residents not as fortunate as himself.

▲

Housing Minister Yvette Cooper,
visited the Manor Estate at Toll
Bar, to inspect the damage caused
by the floods. She is pictured here
taking a look inside resident
Sharon Sanderson's home.

▶

Yvette Cooper discusses the
situation with Pat Hagan, Toll Bar
Neighbourhood manager.

Sharon Sanderson's
Manor Estate home has
suffered badly in the
floods.

WORKSOP AND SURROUNDING AREA

Not for decades, has anyone seen anything quite like the floods that hit Bassetlaw and Rotherham in June this year. A month's worth of rain fell in one night and, with almost no warning, our towns, villages and homes were flooded, one after another.

Last ditch attempts to stop the rising water in its tracks were useless, as eventually we realised the scale of what was happening. Emergency services were stretched to the limit. Fire crews were evacuating streets of people at a time, while police attempted to keep order in towns filled with panicked people.

In Worksop, the town centre had become a lake overnight, and people living on Central Avenue and the surrounding streets were forced to abandon their homes. There was more misery in Retford, as many woke up to find their homes and gardens immersed.

In the town's leisure centre, evacuees were taken to recuperate from their ordeal, comforted by council staff who had been working throughout the night. In Dinnington and Laughton Common there was a similar story, families were up all night bailing out water, and were stood assessing the damage as the sun came up.

But there was a bigger threat to come – Ulley Reservoir. Overnight, the nation's eyes had turned to South Yorkshire. The dam was in danger of bursting, and a massive operation was set up by the police to avert, what could have turned out to be a total disaster. The M1 was closed, causing traffic chaos and emergency efforts to evacuate those most at risk began.

People from Treeton, Catcliffe and Whiston had to flee their homes – taking refuge at Dinnington Comprehensive School, where the national media was waiting. As the week went on, everyone held their breath waiting for news. Rumours flew round daily that Ulley had burst – to the relief of everyone, it never happened.

But behind the headlines, and underneath the hysteria were real stories, happening to real people. And it's those people who are the main characters in this piece. The people who helped bail out a friend, the people who drove round looking for sandbags for elderly neighbours, the people who took in those who had nowhere else to go.

The term 'community spirit' is tossed around a lot these days, and is perhaps not enough to describe how everyone pulled together. Many pensioners said it reminded them of the war years – some might say there is no better tribute to how much the people of Bassetlaw and Rotherham did for one another.

Yes, sandbags were in short supply, homes were being ruined one after another, and no-one knew when it was going to end, but everyone kept going and carried on bailing.

However, it is easy to be fooled by pictures of children splashing round in the water, and of hardy old women leaning on mops as they swept out their wrecked homes – because amidst it all was heartache.

Once the waters had gone, and with the crisis over – people were faced with the reality of how much they had lost. For days skips lined the streets as people threw away ruined belongings. Some threw out everything they owned.

Vulnerable people were the worst hit – those living alone, the elderly, and those with no insurance, with no means of replacing what they had lost. Outside the houses, people tried to be seen as 'making the best of it', but inside, there were tears, as they counted the cost. It was a lonely time for many.

Now, those who escaped the floods look back on what happened in June 2007, as a mad week, or a good story to tell. But for those who are still living in temporary homes, or in houses with no carpets or wallpaper, the consequences of what happened go on.

However they have not been forgotten, a relief fund has been set up by the Government, and locally, charity flood appeals have been raising money for those badly-affected.

Looking back, everyone has their own memories, which will forever define the flood for them – bad and good. It might be of being rescued, having to throw out a treasured possession, returning home and seeing the damage for the first time, or finding help from an unexpected quarter.

And all of them will last a lifetime.

DINNINGTON & MALTBY EDITION   Friday 29th June 2007   www.dinningtonguardian.co.uk   **55p** (62p home delivered)

Guardian

Get ready for Baby Of The Year **p20**	Two die in road tragedy **p9**	Darren & Lilia in Todwick **p10**

Covering: Dinnington • Maltby • Anston • Aston • Thurcroft • Kiveton • Todwick • Wales • Swallownest • Hellaby • Thorpe Salvin • Woodsetts • Harthill • Woodall • Ulley • Laughton

DAM DRAMA

- **Villages near Ulley dam evacuated**
- **Homes wrecked by raging torrents**
- **More heavy rain to come**

Special reports and pictures pages 2,3,4&5

▲

The King Edward Pub with water lapping at the door.

◄

Kids splashing through the flood water on Bridge Street, Worksop.

▲
A surprisingly deserted Central Avenue, Worksop.

▶
The traffic lights are on red but the only 'traffic' moving along Bridge Street are pedestrians.

▲
Many shops along
Bridge Street were
forced to close.

◀

There is no-one to
linger on the
Bridge Street
benches as this
normally busy
thoroughfare has
become eerily
quiet.

▲
This lone cyclist makes his way along Ryton Street past the Royal Mail depot.

▶

Waters are getting dangerously high as this car battles through floods on Central Avenue.

▲

The waters fail to part for this motorist on Newcastle Avenue, Worksop.

◄

People stand in amazement at the flood waters on Newcastle Avenue, while others try to make their way along the street.

Local girls roll-up
their trousers
and brave the
flood waters
along Newcastle
Avenue.

▶

Police close the
roads as sections
become
impassable along
Newcastle
Avenue.

▲

Portland School pupils make their way home through the flooded Worksop town centre.

◄

Dinnington Comprehensive School on Doe Quarry Lane was used as an evacuation centre.

Families sleep on blow-up beds and sleeping bags as they wait to hear some news about their homes.

▶

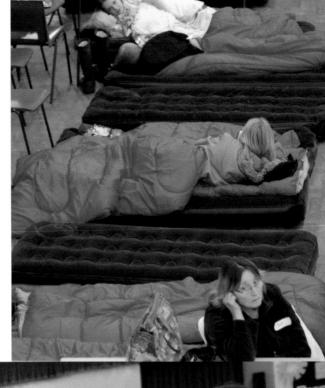

▼

RMBC Social Services workers organise the centre at Dinnington Comprehensive School.

▲
Police stationed outside the school helping to coordinate the flood relief for local residents.

◄
Andrew Roddison, Tenant Representative, outside Dinnington Comprehensive School.

▲

A GMTV news crew on site at Dinnington Comprehensive School covering the impact the floods had on local communities.

▶

Local residents wait anxiously to discover any news about being able to return to their homes and take stock of the damage.

▲

Swollen from the recent downpours, Ulley Reservoir cannot take any more water.

◀

Police close off pathways down to the reservoir as water levels get dangerously high.

▲
Emergency services wait for further developments at Ulley Reservoir.

▶
Schoolchildren look on as a man films the history-making scenes.

Carlton Mill pond breaks its banks.

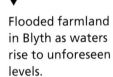

Flooded farmland in Blyth as waters rise to unforeseen levels.

Landslide at Goldthorpe Mill, Oldcotes, following flooding.

▶

▼

The river that runs through Blyth rages beneath the bridge that forms the main road.

▲

Kerry Neale wades through Priorswell Road after collecting daughter Isobel from the Alphabet Day Nursery which closed its doors due to rising flood waters.

◄

June Butterfield, a resident of Priorswell Road, plays the waiting game to see if the flood waters will rise or fall.

▲   Priorswell Road junction with Shelley Street under water following floods.

▶

Shelley Street flooding is relieved slightly when residents at Rose Cottage broke holes through their garden wall to let the flood waters divert through their garden.

▲
Drying time!

▶

Vulnerable areas of Barratt Motors are boarded up in the hope that it will keep the waters at bay.

◀

Sandbags are brought in for the Reef nightclub, Worksop.

▼

Allen Street was completely flooded with water nearly reaching the ground floor windows of houses.

▲

Residents tried to
hold back the
waters with
home-made
barricades but to
no avail as the
muddy waters
pushed past.

▶

Scenes of
devastation as
waters finally
enter the houses
on Allen Street.

▲

Destruction in the
living room of
Roger Stocks'
Allen Street home.

◄

Submerged cones
on Central Avenue
give an indication
as to water levels.

A sorry sight: Worksop's Cricket and Sports Club – and in contrast, how the ground looks without any flood water.

Joanne Bolsover in her back garden, Donstone, Dinnington.

▶

▼

Kids continue to play in the streets, Donstone, Dinnington floods.

▲

A never before seen view of Hardy Street, Worksop, but there is no one waiting at this bus stop.

◄

Donstone, Dinnington floods.

▲

Aerial views of
Ulley Country Park
flooded.

▶

Emergency
services lined up
along the road at
Ulley Country
Park.

▲
An aerial view of Worksop town centre showing the extent of the flooding. Newcastle Avenue (leading to town centre), Central Avenue, Cricket Ground (top), Hardy Street, Allen Street.

◀
Flooded: The Canch, Priory Church and Worksop Library.

Central Avenue,
Cricket Ground
(bottom) and Ryton
Street from the air.

▼

Workers splashing
around on Ryton
Street, Worksop.

▲

Under water the
road beneath the
railway bridge at
Clarborough.

◀

Church Lane,
Retford completely
flooded.

▲

Riding down Main Street, (between
Retford and Gainsborough),
Clarborough.

▶

Greenwoods, Bridge Street, Worksop.
Left to right are Graham Phillips (relief
manager) and Debbie Ashley (sales
assistant) mopping out the shop.

▲

Emergency
Services discuss
the best options
to cope with
recent flooding
at Ulley Country
Park.

◄

The Fire Service
offered relief to
many people
during the recent
floods.

▲
Many of the main high street stores had to remain closed due to the rise in water levels.

▶

Staff at Worksop stores kept their spirits up as the clean-up began.

Morrisons store with flood waters running perilously close.

River banks burst
and the flood
waters engulf
the pathways.

▶

Water levels rise
high enough to
almost cover
bridges over the
river.

▲
Police close off the bridges as the river water threatens to engulf the walkway.

◄
Access to Riverside Walk is closed off by police.

Many local people volunteered their time in order to help neighbours.

▶

▼

A game of football is impossible, perhaps the sport should be water polo!

▲
The water has risen almost to this basketball hoop.

◀
Walking the dog!

▲
School kids have a whale of a time as they splash through the flood waters.

▶
The celebrations are over as the flood waters swamp Donstone, Dinnington.

Clear up after the floods on Allen Street.

◄

▼

Mandy Elliott surveying the damage the floods have caused in her home on Allen Street.

▶

Joanne
Bolsolver's house
was badly
damaged by the
floods,
Donstone,
Dinnington.

▼

Joanne
Bolsolver's house
during the
floods.